Opening Our Hearts

Opening Our Hearts

by
DAVID H. ROSEN

RESOURCE *Publications* • Eugene, Oregon

OPENING OUR HEARTS

Resource Publications
An Imprint of Wipf and Stock Publishers
199 W. 8th Ave., Suite 3
Eugene, OR 97401

www.wipfandstock.com

PAPERBACK ISBN: 978-1-6667-5505-3
HARDCOVER ISBN: 978-1-6667-5506-0
EBOOK ISBN: 978-1-6667-5507-7

VERSION NUMBER 091922

ALSO BY DAVID H. ROSEN

Henry's Tower (children's book) (Platypus Books, 1984)

Medicine as a Human Experience (With David Reiser) (introduction to clinical issues) (University Park Press, 1984), (Aspen Systems, 1985)

Transforming Depression: Healing the Soul through Creativity (Putnam, 1993) (Penguin Group, 1996) (Nicholas-Hays, 2002)

The Tao of Jung: The Way of Integrity (Penguin Group, 1996) (Wipf & Stock Publishers, 2019)

The Tao of Elvis (Harcourt, 2002) (Wipf and Stock, 2013)

Clouds and More Clouds (collection of haiku) (Lily Pool Press, 2013)

The Healing Spirit of Haiku (With Joel Weishaus) (haiku & dialogue between two old friends) (North Atlantic Books, 2004), (Resource Publications, an Imprint of Wipf and Stock Publishers, 2014)

Lost in the Long White Cloud: Finding My Way Home (1st memoir) (Wipf and Stock, 2014)

Time, Love and Licorice: A Healing Coloring Storybook (Wipf and Stock, 2015)

Darkness Holding Light (collection of poems) (edited by David H. Rosen and Carol Goodman) (Resource Publications, 2016)

Spelunking Through Life (collection of haiku) (Resource Publications, 2016)

Living with Evergreens (collection of haiku) (Resource Publications, 2016)

In Search of the Hidden Pond (collection of haiku) (Resource Publications, 2016)

Less Is More: A Collection of Ten-Minute Plays (edited by David H. Rosen with two of his own plays) (Resource Publications, 2016)

White Rose, Red Rose (With Johnny Baranski) (collection of haiku & dialogue between the authors) (Resource Publications, 2017)

Patient-Centered Medicine: A Human Experience (with Uyen Hoang) (introduction to clinical principles and issues) (Oxford University Press, 2017)

The Alchemy of Cooking: Recipes with a Jungian Twist (Wipf and Stock, 2017)

Samantha the Sleuth & Zack's Hard Lesson (children's book) (Resource Publications, 2018)

Opal Whiteley's Beginning and Hoops & Hoopla (historical fiction and personal story)(Resource Publications, 2018)

Torii Haiku: Profane to a Sacred Life (collection of haiku) (Resource Publications, 2018)

Look Closely (collection of haiku) (Resource Publications, 2019)

Warming to Gold (collection of haiku) (Resource Publications, 2019)

Kindergarten Symphony: An ABC Book (children's book) (Resource Publications, 2019)

Lesbianism: A Father-Daughter Conversation (With Rachel Rosen) (treatise on lesbianism) (Resource Publications, 2019)

Every Day is a Good Day (collection of haiku) (Resource Publications, 2020)

Soul Circles: Mandalas and Meaning (With Jeremy Jensen) (clinical treatise with artist analysand) (Resource Publications, 2020)

Torn Asunder: Putting Back the Pieces (2nd memoir) (Resource Publications, 2020)

Soul to Soul: Aphorisms for Life (philosophical work) (Resource Publications, 2021)

In addition, Rosen edited and wrote the forewords for the first 20 volumes of the Fay Book Series in Analytical Psychology (1991–2017). The complete series is listed in the Appendix.

Rosen has also performed comedy at the Tiny Tavern and the Green Room in Eugene, Oregon. You can watch his performances on YouTube by typing in the following: "Dr. Nada Live at the Tiny Tavern" https://www.youtube.com/watch?v=0TUSNrU7f7A , "Dr. Nada Live at Tiny Tavern Part II" https://www.youtube.com/watch?v=xQXnfhYThs4 , and "Dr. Nada Live at the Green Room" https://www.youtube.com/watch?v=s0zvmNqD57Q&t=270s

"Wisdom begins in wonder"
-Socrates

Preface

This collection of little poems, including haiku, is the eleventh I've penned. They were written over several years. Haiku expresses healing moments, which has always drawn me to this form of poetry. I thank God and Sophia for free verse and these little poems that express big ideas.

Ember...
first granddaughter
opening our hearts

Surprise surprise...
how am I?
still alive

Love is real
in solitude &
relationship

Father's parents...
from Romania
married forever

Darkness...
every haiku
a shooting star

Red and white
rhododendrons...
I, too, blossom

When I pray...
remembering
Mount Koya

Blue jeans
blue sky...
the blues

Lanara once said,
"Your bed
is like a cloud."

Reserved parking
for those who want
reserved parking

On the bench...
waiting for
Godot

In the garden
roses, peaches...
even asparagus

Soul symbol...
this sphere
of light

Three paintings...
glimpses of
reality

Slug trail
on the porch...
now, I understand my life

Fresh mowed grass
blooming roses...
my nose works overtime

At the post office
for mail...
with my female

What happened?
a fall...
so I crawl

Talked to Lolly
her cancer is back...
see you in heaven

Staring at the wall
not Zen, but
there's a hole

Looking at the hole
have I stumbled
into no-self?

For my gravestone:
    being still
    still being

Clouds of pollen
drift by...
a goddess

Here I am
here I stand
in Holy Land

Tops of fir trees
swaying...
sound of rain

Oregon sunshine
lavender...
oh, Cezanne

Walking slowly...
the sun
sets slowly

Moonrise...
opens
our hearts

Rhododendron
blooms...
birdsong

Divorce...
peeling
a yellow onion

Hey death...
the door
is open

Graveyard
crows...
a murder

Am I morbid?
no...
just 77

Never went...
so I wrote
Kindergarten Symphony

A snake?
yes...
ouroboros

Fathers'
Purple Heart...
bless, bless

Fell again...
cried and asked God
for help

Foggy morning...
walking
this cloud

Life moves to death...
death moves to
life

Walking
in a cloud...
an angel?

I know...
what do I know?
nothing

Bamboo
for you...
a haiku?

Sitting by the
garden...
kinship with roses

Alone...
all
One

An opening
tulip...
our love

Threw a lemon
into the pond...
lemonade?

Red dragonfly
comes to visit...
alone, yet not

Sunrise,
sunset...
same

Sauntering around a monastery's lake,
a sign appeared:

Walking on water
prohibited...
monks only

On a bench with Lanara...
four years later
marriage

Sweeping
the porch...
refreshing

Wisdom
in dreams...
truth be told

Growing up
growing down...
evergreen

Retired early,
but still
tired

Long life
short death...
afterlife

Clouds and
more clouds...
lone raven

I'm a grasshopper
but I can't jump
anymore

Texas doctor died...
reborn
in Oregon

The scent
of peppermint...
first snow

Evening walk...
my companion,
an owl

Opening
our hearts...
evening of joy